Unleashing Your Ruth

A Journey of Faith,
Courage,
and Divine Purpose

By Pastor Beth Kelley

Copyright

Copyright © 2024 Pastor Beth Kelley

Publisher: Kindle Direct Publishing
ISBN: 9798339483618
Library of Congress Control Number: [LCCN]
Printed in the United States of America
First Edition: 2024
Cover Design: Beth Kelley
Author Photograph: Callen Kelley

Scripture quotations are taken from the Holy Bible, New Living Translation (NLT), copyright © 1996, 2004, 2015 by Tyndale House Foundation. Used by permission of Tyndale House Publishers, Inc., Carol Stream, Illinois 60188. All rights reserved.

This book is a work of nonfiction. While all attempts have been made to verify the information provided in this publication, the author and publisher assume no responsibility for errors, omissions, or contrary interpretations of the subject matter herein. The views expressed in this book are those of the author alone and should not be considered professional advice. The reader should consult a professional where appropriate.

Dedication:

To all the women of faith who strive to walk in the fullness of God's purpose for their lives. May this book inspire and empower you to embrace your unique calling and overcome every obstacle with grace and strength.

Contact Information:

For more information, please visit Pastor Beth Kelley at PastorBethKelley@gmail.com.

Follow us on social media: YouTube: JIGSAWPastorBeth@JIGSAWPastorBeth

Table of content

Chapter 1

The Roar and Rise of a Ruth

Ruth's story is one of incredible dedication, sacrifice, and faithfulness. Her journey from Moab to Bethlehem shows us how God can take someone from a place of rescue to a place of restoration. Ruth was courageous, bold, and willing to step into the unknown, leaving her comfort zone behind to walk in unity with God's plan. This is what it means to have the "Character of a Ruth" — to be brave, faith-filled, and determined, even in the midst of chaos.

The first trait we see in Ruth is her loyalty to God. Loyalty is more than just a feeling; it is a steadfast decision to stay in God's presence, listen to His voice, and obey Him no matter what. Ruth shows us what it looks like to have a deep devotion to God. Her faith was unshakeable, her commitment unwavering. She understood that God's guidance is worth more than any earthly security.

Ruth was also an example of complete submission to the Holy Spirit. In the Bible, Jesus promised us a Helper — the Holy Spirit — who is our comforter, advocate, counselor, and strengthener (John 14:16-17 "And I will ask the Father, and he will give you another Advocate, who will never leave you. He is the Holy Spirit, who leads into all truth. The world cannot receive him because it isn't looking for him and doesn't recognize him. But you know him, because he lives with you now and later will be in you."). Ruth accepted the guidance of this Helper, allowing the Spirit of Truth to lead her every step of the way. She yielded to God's will, knowing that He alone could direct her path.

A key part of Ruth's character was her honor and virtue. She was known for her moral excellence, a woman who was honest, righteous, and upright in all her dealings. Ruth wasn't just good in theory; she lived out these qualities daily. Her life was a testament to the power of living with integrity and virtue.

Ruth also demonstrated the importance of forming covenant friendships and strategic alliances. She developed deep connections with both men and women who were committed to moving God's kingdom forward. Ruth's bond with Naomi, her mother-in-law, was not just a friendship; it was a covenant relationship based on mutual respect, love, and loyalty. She also forged an alliance with Boaz, which was a strategic partnership blessed by God.

Ruth had the courage to leave her past behind and embrace a new future. She was a barrier-breaker, a woman who wasn't afraid to face new cultures, people, or challenges. She welcomed everyone with open arms, showing kindness like a flower drawing bees to nectar. Ruth's heart for others made people want to know more about the God she served.

Another powerful trait of Ruth was her humility. She was willing to submit and obey God's plan, even when it wasn't easy. When Naomi gave her instructions, Ruth responded, "I will do everything you say" (Ruth 3:5 "I will do everything you say," Ruth replied.). This shows her willingness to follow God's will, no matter where it led her.

Ruth wasn't just a woman of words; she was a woman of action. She knew that declarations were meaningless without follow-through. Ruth was strategic, discerning when to speak and when to act. She aligned herself with God's will, understanding that sometimes it's more important to walk in faith than to talk about it.

However, Ruth had her challenges. She had to be aware of hijackers that could derail her journey. Idleness, cultural biases like racism, sexism, and classism, selfishness, and fear of the future could all have kept her from stepping into her destiny. But Ruth stayed focused on God, refusing to be held back by these obstacles.

Ruth's strength came from her inner character. She was humble, not shy; she was filled with faith, committed to seeing things through. Ruth understood her destiny and embraced it fully. She tapped into the powerful seed of purpose that God had placed within her, allowing it to grow and flourish.

Behind every Ruth is a Naomi, a mentor who sharpens, teaches, and guides. Naomi played a critical role in Ruth's life, helping her to grow in wisdom and grace. Ruth listened carefully to Naomi's advice, following her directions to the letter. She worked hard, remained meek, yet strong, and developed the ability to think ahead for the good of others.

Women of God are called to rise up in their Ruth anointing. Our communities, cities, states, and nations need women of stability, perseverance, and moral integrity. Just as Ruth came alongside Boaz, women today are called to stand with and support those around them, providing love, strength, and protection.

Ruth also had a unique role as a generational protectress. She carried the ability to raise the next generation with fierce love, motivation, and care. As the Bible says in Proverbs 22:6, "Train up a child in the way he should go, and when he is old, he will not depart from it."the NLT version says, "Direct your children onto the right path, and when they are older, they will not leave it." Ruth embodied this principle, leading by example and standing up for what is right.

Ruth was positioned by God as a protector. She was always ready to stand her ground, full of righteous intuition and spiritual insight. She was prepared to act when needed, guided by her deep connection with God.

But even with all these qualities, Ruth still faced opposition. One danger was getting ahead of God, trying to move forward without His direction. To be effective in her calling, Ruth had to stay close to God, seeking healing and deliverance from anything that could hold her back, like fear, anger, bitterness, or grief.

Ruth demonstrated love and honor in all she did. She didn't get caught up in the trappings of success or worldly recognition. Instead, she committed every day to the service of Jesus Christ, seeking His will above all else.

God is calling each of us to engage with Him and embrace the encounter. He awakens the deepest parts of our hearts, bringing to light things we need to release or heal. When we let go of what He tells us to let go, we become filled with His power, authority, and purpose.

When we follow God's call, our faces become like flint, unmovable and unshakable (Isaiah 50:7 "Because the Sovereign Lord helps me, I will not be disgraced. Therefore, I have set my face like a stone, determined to do his will. And I know that I will not be put to shame."). We know what we need to do, and no fear, no mountains, and no giants can stop us. This is the courage and faith of a Ruth.

God doesn't always show us the entire plan upfront. He wants us to be willing to step out in faith, saying, "Send me, I will go," even when we don't know the end result. This kind of trust and obedience is what sets a Ruth apart.

Are you ready to rise like Ruth? Are you ready to embrace your calling, to be bold, courageous, and faith-filled, no matter what lies ahead? God is calling you to step into your destiny. Engage with Him, embrace the encounter, and let Him lead you on an incredible journey of faith.

Chapter 2

A Set Time for Your Destiny

There is a set time for your destiny. Scripture reminds us that God has planted something in each of us that, in its due season, will blossom into our divine purpose and plan. When we become aware that something bigger is at work within us, we are ignited by a force that can face any opposition. The Bible is filled with verses that speak to this idea —

that God has a perfect time for everything and everyone.

Galatians 6:9 (AMP) encourages us not to grow weary in doing good, for at the proper time, we will reap a harvest if we do not give up. This is a reminder that perseverance is key when waiting for our destiny to unfold. The NLT version says, "So let's not get tired of doing what is good. At just the right time we will reap a harvest of blessing if we don't give up." **Ecclesiastes 3:10** "I have seen the burden God has placed on us all." speaks of how God has given us the burden of time, but also the beauty of His timing. **Habakkuk 2:3** "This vision is for a future time. It describes the end, and it will be fulfilled. If it seems slow in coming, wait patiently, for it will surely take place. It will not be delayed." tells us that the vision is for an appointed time, and though it may seem slow in coming, we are to wait for it, for it will surely come to pass. **Isaiah 46:10** "Only I can tell you the future before it even happens. Everything I plan will come to pass, for I do whatever I wish." This scripture assures us that

God knows the end from the beginning, and His purpose will stand. **Jeremiah 1:5** "I knew you before I formed you in your mother's womb. Before you were born I set you apart and appointed you as my prophet to the nations." It reminds us that God knew us before we were formed in the womb and set us apart for His plans. Lastly, **Proverbs 20:24** "The Lord directs our steps, so why try to understand everything along the way?" This tells us that a person's steps are directed by the Lord. Together, these scriptures show that God's timing is perfect and purposeful.

When we become aware that God has planted something greater within us, our awareness ignites a force to face any opposition. This awareness anchors us to the vision, increases our faith exponentially, and gives us abundant courage to walk in God's plans. Taking that first step of faith unlocks and releases the provision, favor, and resources needed to fulfill our God-given vision.

However, many things try to steal our God vision. Often, the greatest giants we fight are in our own minds. Grief from the loss of a loved one, job, or relationship can try to hold us back. Poverty and a mindset of lack make us believe we will never have enough. Social pressure from friends and family and cultural customs or traditions can make us doubt the new path God is leading us on. The enemy often tells us the lie that "I don't have enough" to stop us from moving forward.

Life's hardships, troubles, and tribulations can either motivate us or cause us to shut down. Our destiny is wrapped up in our motivation to keep going. If we allow complacency to take root, our destiny can wither and die. God placed a seed of destiny within each of us because He knows what motivates us. The enemy may try to lie to us, saying we're not going anywhere, but we have the choice to move our destiny out of the muck and mire.

Consider a mother's sacrifice. There is no mother who would not try to move heaven and earth for her children. A mother's love is eternal, whether her children are young or old. When a mother accepts another child as her own, that child receives the same tenacity, love, prayers, and encouragement as any biological child. This is what Naomi did for Ruth. Ruth accepted Naomi as her mother, vowing to go where Naomi went, live where Naomi lived, die where Naomi died, and accept Naomi's God as her own.

Ruth's commitment was not just a promise; it was a deep, heartfelt oath. Through her trials and grief, Ruth found her identity in God. She swore four oaths: to go wherever Naomi led, to sleep wherever Naomi laid her head, to die in the place where Naomi took her last breath, and to embrace Naomi's God as her own. Her commitment to her husband was not just to him but to his entire bloodline, including his mother, Naomi. This was a covenant commitment, extending even unto death.

God offers us redemption and rescue. Our redemption is a precious gift from God. It is He alone who helps us step over every obstacle in our walk with Him. Through redemption, God changes our hearts and uses our lives to rescue others,

showing them His marvelous love and grace
through our example.

Where would we be without God's redemption?
Without it, we would be lost, forgotten, scattered,
and face an eternity separated from God. But God,
in His great love, rescues us from ourselves. When
He rescues us, we become redeemed — given a
second chance time after time. We become devoted,
with our devotion being earned through the sacrifice
of His eternal love. We are healed, no longer broken
or forgotten. We are delivered from the lies of the
enemy, renewed, restored, and made whole again.

Ruth's words echo this truth. In Ruth 1:16, she
declares, "Where you go, I will go; where you live,
I will live. Your people will be my people, and your
God will be my God." Her commitment was an act
of faith, showing that she was ready to follow
wherever God would lead her.

When God rescues us, He gives us new
opportunities to align our lives with His purpose.
We begin to see ourselves differently — as

valuable, chosen, and called. We recognize that God has placed a destiny inside of us that is meant to grow and flourish in His perfect timing.

Remember, God's timing is always perfect. We may not see the full picture now, but God has a set time for everything. The vision He has planted in you will come to pass if you do not give up. Keep walking in faith, trusting that God is directing your steps and leading you toward His divine purpose for your life.

Scriptures for more in-depth study:

Psalm 37:5
"Commit everything you do to the Lord. Trust him, and he will help you."

Philippians 4:13
"For I can do everything through Christ, who gives me strength."

1 Corinthians 15:58
"So, my dear brothers and sisters, be strong and

immovable. Always work enthusiastically for the Lord, for you know that nothing you do for the Lord is ever useless."

Romans 12:2
"Don't copy the behavior and customs of this world, but let God transform you into a new person by changing the way you think. Then you will learn to know God's will for you, which is good and pleasing and perfect."

Colossians 3:23-24
"Work willingly at whatever you do, as though you were working for the Lord rather than for people. Remember that the Lord will give you an inheritance as your reward, and that the Master you are serving is Christ."

James 1:5
"If you need wisdom, ask our generous God, and he will give it to you. He will not rebuke you for asking."

Proverbs 3:5-6

"Trust in the Lord with all your heart; do not depend on your own understanding. Seek his will in all you do, and he will show you which path to take."

Matthew 6:33

"Seek the Kingdom of God above all else, and live righteously, and he will give you everything you need."

2 Corinthians 12:9

"Each time he said, 'My grace is all you need. My power works best in weakness.' So now I am glad to boast about my weaknesses, so that the power of Christ can work through me."

Chapter 3

Leaving What Is Familiar Is Not Walking in the Wilderness

Leaving what is familiar is not the same as wandering aimlessly in the wilderness. Sometimes, God calls us to step away from what we know —

old mindsets, patterns of behavior, or even close relationships — so that He can guide us into something new and greater. Leaving behind what is comfortable may feel like a loss, but it is actually a step toward embracing the new adventures that God has for us.

We may need to leave behind certain ways of thinking, habits, or even family and friends who might unintentionally hold us back from reaching our full potential. For example, God got my attention after the third rear-end car accident, which forced me to give up a career I loved as an occupational therapist. I had to change my mindset and my behaviors to become who I am today. It wasn't that I stopped loving those around me, but I realized that staying in those old relationships might limit both my growth and theirs. By separating for a time, we all have the chance to grow.

This separation sharpens our focus and increases our motivation. It gives us the space to see clearly what God wants for us and to pursue it with all our hearts. But stepping out of what is familiar can feel like a huge risk, and it often brings fears to the surface.

Fear is one of the biggest things that holds us back from embracing new adventures. We might fear the unknown, worry that we won't have enough provision, or be afraid of being alone. We may even fear what God will ask of us when we are alone with Him. These fears can feel overwhelming, but they don't have to stop us.

Doubt is another enemy we face. We might start to believe lies like, "You can't do that," "You're not smart enough," or "No one will listen to you." These lies can keep us stuck, afraid to move forward into the new things God has for us. We need to remember that these negative thoughts are not from God.

To combat fear and doubt, we must turn to God's Word. We need to read it, believe it, and speak it out loud. Speaking the truth of God's Word changes the atmosphere around us. When we declare His promises over our lives, we stop the enemy in his tracks. We call in God's love where there is hate, provision where there is lack, and confidence where there is doubt. The Bible says in **1 John 4:18** "Such love has no fear because perfect love expels all fear. If we are afraid, it is for fear of punishment, and this shows that we have not fully experienced his perfect love."

We also need to say "yes" to God. This means yielding to His will, submitting to His guidance, honoring His word, and putting on the full armor of God every day. This is like getting dressed in the morning. It might mean going through training or even a kind of spiritual "boot camp" to clean out old ways of thinking and kick out the squatters of negative thoughts.

Trusting God with every part of our being is essential. The "Ruth anointing" is about total, complete trust, even when we don't know what lies ahead. God knows, and we can trust that His plans for us are good, even if we would hesitate if we knew the full journey in advance. As **Proverbs 3:5-6** says, "Trust in the Lord with all your heart; do not depend on your own understanding. Seek his will in all you do, and he will show you which path to take."

Cutting ourselves free from the past allows us to find God in the spaces in between. When we submit to Him, He can change our perspective and help us see the path He wants us to take clearly. This process may not be easy, but it is necessary to move forward.

We must not stop moving forward. Stopping can kill everything tied to our destiny, purpose, and the plans God has for our lives. Remember, you are enough for God to use, mold, and place in His refining fire to purify and prepare you for your calling. God has more for you, so do not stop!

Let's fill in the blanks: **[Your Name Here]** succeeded because she said "yes" to God. She was willing to learn and obey. **[Your Name Here]** excels because she listens to her mentors — the Father, the Son Jesus, and the Holy Spirit, as well as the earthly mentors God placed in her path. Listen to them, and willingly receive godly counsel to stay on the right road.

Developing an inner circle of influence is important. Surround yourself with people who know and understand God's call on your life. They should be committed to walking alongside you, listening for God's direction, and studying His Word. As **Proverbs 11:14** says, "Without wise leadership, a nation falls; there is safety in having many advisers." Another translation reads,"Where there is no guidance, a people falls, but in an abundance of counselors there is safety."

We must have a "different spirit" — not one of worldliness but of godliness. Caleb and Joshua had this different spirit when they spied out the land of giants and chose to believe God's promises, unlike the other ten spies who reported doom and gloom. God honored their faith and confirmed their truth.

Ruth also had a "different spirit." Even though she was a Moabite and not a Jew, God's Spirit was in her. She listened to Naomi, her mentor, and declared, "Your God shall be my God." Ruth activated her "different spirit" through her confession, just as Caleb and Joshua did in the land of giants.

When we say, "He said it, I believe it, that's enough for me," we set into motion events that God has ordained. We all have access to God's promises, but it is our choice whether to say "yes" or "no." Remember, a "yes" to God opens doors that no man, nor Satan, can shut!

Scriptures for Further Study:

Psalm 32:8
"The Lord says, 'I will guide you along the best pathway for your life. I will advise you and watch over you.'"

Isaiah 43:18-19
"But forget all that — it is nothing compared to what I am going to do. For I am about to do something new. See, I have already begun! Do you not see it? I will make a pathway through the

wilderness. I will create rivers in the dry
wasteland."

Romans 8:28

"And we know that God causes everything to work
together for the good of those who love God and are
called according to his purpose for them."

Joshua 1:9

"This is my command—be strong and courageous!
Do not be afraid or discouraged. For the Lord your
God is with you wherever you go."

Philippians 4:6-7

"Don't worry about anything; instead, pray about
everything. Tell God what you need, and thank him
for all he has done. Then you will experience God's
peace, which exceeds anything we can understand.
His peace will guard your hearts and minds as you
live in Christ Jesus."

Isaiah 41:10

"Don't be afraid, for I am with you. Don't be
discouraged, for I am your God. I will strengthen

you and help you. I will hold you up with my
victorious right hand."

Psalm 37:23-24
"The Lord directs the steps of the godly. He delights
in every detail of their lives. Though they stumble,
they will never fall, for the Lord holds them by the
hand."

Hebrews 12:1
"Therefore, since we are surrounded by such a huge
crowd of witnesses to the life of faith, let us strip off
every weight that slows us down, especially the sin
that so easily trips us up. And let us run with
endurance the race God has set before us."

Deuteronomy 31:6
"So be strong and courageous! Do not be afraid
and do not panic before them. For the Lord your
God will personally go ahead of you. He will
neither fail you nor abandon you."

Ephesians 6:10-11
"A final word: Be strong in the Lord and in his

mighty power. Put on all of God's armor so that you will be able to stand firm against all strategies of the devil."

Chapter 4

Bitterness Turns to Delight and Contentment

God gives us a living example in the story of Ruth and Naomi of how He redeems and restores our losses, griefs, hurts, troubles, and pain. He compensates us for what the enemy has stolen, returning to us peace, joy, love, fruitfulness, compassion, contentment, and growth. There are times when we are faced with what we see as amazing opportunities or what looks like a way out of impossible situations. We might want to take these opportunities, but we must be careful. If it's just a "good" opportunity and not a "God" opportunity, it could lead us away from God's plan.

To discern the difference, we must ask the Holy Spirit for guidance and confirmation. How do we do this? By praying, and then praying some more. We must wait patiently, quietly, and expectantly for God's answer. Once we receive it, we can make our decision confidently, without rushing ahead and finding ourselves in deep water. If we do make a wrong choice, repentance will bring us back to safety, but there may still be a mess to clean up. Remember, not every opportunity is from God.

Elimelech, Naomi's husband, made this mistake. He took his family out of Judah to Moab to escape a famine, thinking it was a good idea. For a while, it may have seemed like things would work out, but Scripture tells us that Elimelech and his two sons died in Moab. They broke their covenant with God, and the sons married women from an idolatrous nation. They had no children, possibly because of their sin. But God wasn't finished with Naomi. Even in her loss, Naomi set a powerful example for her daughters-in-law, Ruth and Orpah. Through Naomi's influence, Ruth, a woman from a pagan nation, repented, rejected idol worship, and accepted the Lord as her God. God received her repentance and gave her a new beginning with Boaz. Ruth's deliverance literally led to the birth of the bloodline that brought forth Christ.

Naomi's strength was deeply rooted in the Lord. How do we know this? Because she chose to leave Moab and return to Judah. She could have given up and stayed in the wilderness, but she didn't. She could have sent Ruth back to her family, but she chose not to. Naomi's faithfulness in returning to God's land showed her trust in Him, even in the midst of her pain.

Naomi also recognized God's hand of protection. She gave Ruth specific instructions on the journey back to Judah, showing her awareness of God's guidance. Naomi was flexible and willing to be led by the Holy Spirit, always staying in a position where God could direct her steps.

But where did bitterness enter Naomi's heart? It came with the death of her husband and then her two sons. When Naomi returned to Bethlehem, she openly confessed her bitterness. She said, "Don't call me Naomi. Instead, call me Mara, for the Almighty has made life very bitter for me" (Ruth 1:20, NLT).

Yet, in her honesty and confession, healing began. Naomi brought her bitterness, hurt, and despair to God. She confessed it all, and according to James 5:16, confession brings healing: *Confess your sins to each other and pray for each other so that you may be healed. The earnest prayer of a righteous person has great power and produces wonderful results.* Through her confession, God began to heal her heart.

Naomi's healing was crucial for the discipleship of Ruth. Naomi had to let go of her bitterness to see God's plan for Ruth come to fruition. She needed to guide Ruth in the ways of the Lord, and she could not do that if she held onto her own pain. Naomi's journey from bitterness to delight and contentment is a testimony of how God can transform our grief into growth and our sorrow into strength.

Scriptures for Further Study:

1. **Ruth 1:20**

   "Don't call me Naomi. Instead, call me Mara, for the Almighty has made life very bitter for me."

2. **James 5:16**

   "Confess your sins to each other and pray for each other so that you may be healed. The earnest prayer of a righteous person has great power and produces wonderful results."

These passages illustrate how God can take our bitterness and turn it into something beautiful, just as He did for Naomi and Ruth. Through their story, we learn the importance of waiting on God's timing, seeking His guidance, and trusting Him through every trial.

Chapter 5

Covenant Binds Us to God Through Adversity

The idea of covenant is at the heart of our relationship with God and with one another. As Proverbs 17:17 says, *"A friend is always loyal, and a brother is born to help in time of need."* A covenant binds us to God, and through that covenant, we form relationships with others that are designed to withstand adversity. God ordains friends who stick closer than a brother, born for those tough times when we need support the most.

Women who are united in purpose, with a single goal and mission, are an unstoppable force. When mature women of God come together, confident and bold in their faith, no enemy wants to face them. As Deuteronomy 32:30 says, *"How could one person chase a thousand of them, and two people put ten thousand to flight, unless their Rock had sold them, unless the Lord had given them up?"* When women are joined in the virtues of Ruth and committed to one another, they are powerful. This strength is multiplied when they stand together, contending with the enemy with God's word and prayer.

When God is in our commitments, who can stand against them? Just like Ruth was loyal to Naomi, we must also be loyal to each other and to God. When we give our word or promise to someone, we should follow through with what we say, not just in our attitudes, but also in our actions. A covenant agreement is more than just words — it is a commitment that binds us to a higher purpose.

Covenant Declaration

Ruth's declaration to Naomi is a powerful example of covenant loyalty and love:

- *"Wherever you go, I will go; wherever you live, I will live. Your people will be my people, and your God will be my God. Where you die, I will die, and there I will be buried. May the Lord punish me severely if I allow anything but death to separate us."* (Ruth 1:16-17, NLT)

This declaration shows an unwavering commitment to another person, a bond that reflects the depth of God's love and loyalty to us. It is a covenant that speaks of honor, loyalty, and a willingness to share in both the joys and the hardships of life.

Commitment of Loyalty: Covenant Agreement

Commitment and loyalty are key components of a covenant relationship. When we say, "Wherever you go, I will go," we are choosing to stand with someone through every circumstance, just as Ruth did with Naomi. This kind of commitment is not based on convenience or personal gain, but on a deep, selfless love that reflects God's heart for His people.

Teamwork Requires:

1. **Honor:** Teamwork begins with honor, which means showing respect for each team member, their positions, their authority, their gifts, and their callings. It means valuing each person and the unique role they play in God's plan.

2. **Purpose:** A team must be aware of its purpose — the reason they gather. For

women in unity, that purpose is to glorify God and to accomplish the mission He has given them.

3. **Measure of Rule:** A good team recognizes the boundaries of their authority and trusts the wisdom of others. It's not a competition to lead; every member is vital to the success of God's plan. Each person plays a unique role, and all are equally important.

4. **Diversity of Gifts and Administration:** A team must submit to and align with the established order. This order is predetermined by the vision God places in the hearts of those who are wholly dedicated to His purposes. Each woman must be sold out for God, fully committed to His plans, and willing to submit to the authority He has set in place.

The Power of Unity in Covenant

When women come together in unity, their combined strength can change families, communities, and even nations. As they honor one another, respect each other's gifts and callings, and work toward a common purpose, they become an unstoppable force for God's kingdom. Their loyalty to God and to each other enables them to protect their relationships and fulfill the purposes that God has ordained for them.

Scriptures for Further Study:

1. **Ecclesiastes 4:9-10**
   "Two people are better off than one, for they can help each other succeed. If one person falls, the other can reach out and help. But someone who falls alone is in real trouble."

2. **Hebrews 10:24-25**

    "Let us think of ways to motivate one another to acts of love and good works. And let us not neglect our meeting together, as some people do, but encourage one another, especially now that the day of his return is drawing near."

3. **Ephesians 4:2-3**

    "Always be humble and gentle. Be patient with each other, making allowance for each other's faults because of your love. Make every effort to keep yourselves united in the Spirit, binding yourselves together with peace."

4. **Colossians 3:14**

    "Above all, clothe yourselves with love, which binds us all together in perfect harmony."

5. **Psalm 133:1**

    "How wonderful and pleasant it is when brothers live together in harmony!"

6. Romans 12:10

"Love each other with genuine affection, and take delight in honoring each other."

7. 1 Corinthians 1:10

"I appeal to you, dear brothers and sisters, by the authority of our Lord Jesus Christ, to live in harmony with each other. Let there be no divisions in the church. Rather, be of one mind, united in thought and purpose."

8. Galatians 6:2

"Share each other's burdens, and in this way obey the law of Christ."

9. John 15:12-13

"This is my commandment: Love each other in the same way I have loved you. There is no greater love than to lay down one's life for one's friends."

10. Philippians 2:2-3

"Then make me truly happy by agreeing wholeheartedly with each other, loving one

another, and working together with one mind and purpose. Don't be selfish; don't try to impress others. Be humble, thinking of others as better than yourselves."

11. **Proverbs 22:11**

   "Whoever loves a pure heart and gracious speech will have the king as a friend."

12. **1 John 4:7**

   "Dear friends, let us continue to love one another, for love comes from God. Anyone who loves is a child of God and knows God."

These scriptures provide a deeper understanding of the importance of unity, love, honor, and covenant relationships within the body of Christ. They emphasize the value of supporting one another, working together for God's purposes, and maintaining strong, loving bonds that reflect God's love to the world.

Chapter 6

Barrier Breaker

To be a barrier breaker means to have a pioneering spirit, a willingness to open new ground and step into new territories with courage and faith. Pioneers do not shrink back; they face challenges head-on, fully embracing their kingdom identity in God. This is the spirit that Ruth had — a spirit that refused to accept limitations and instead sought to break barriers that stood in the way of God's purposes.

The Word of God must be our measuring stick in every situation. It is the ultimate authority, providing us with the direction and guidance we need. Our feelings may mislead us or cause us to waver, but God's Word remains steadfast and true. We must actively pursue God's truth, keeping it at the forefront of our hearts and minds, aligning all our actions and purposes with His will.

Ruths Are Barrier Breakers:

Ruths are not content to simply exist; they are determined to bring change and impact the world around them. They are known for breaking barriers in various areas:

- **Breaking the Back of Poverty:** Ruths are hard workers, willing to go the extra mile to provide for themselves and others. They are humanitarians to the core, driven by compassion and a desire to see everyone have what they need.

- **Breaking the Back of Gender Bias:** Ruths challenge the limitations placed on them by society. They refuse to accept that their gender defines their worth or capability.

- **Breaking the Back of Class Systems:** Ruths see the value in every individual, regardless of social status or background. They are not intimidated by systems that try to separate or diminish people based on wealth or birthright.

- **Breaking the Bank for Economic Breakthrough:** Ruths are resourceful and innovative. They find ways to create opportunities and achieve financial freedom, not just for themselves, but for their families and communities.

How Does Ruth Manifest Breakthrough?

Ruth manifests breakthrough through a combination of godly attributes and determined action:

1. **Decisiveness:** Ruths possess a can-do, pioneering spirit. They make clear decisions and act upon them with confidence. They are not easily swayed by circumstances or doubts, but instead choose to move forward in faith.

2. **Faith:** Faith is essential for breakthrough. As James 1:6 "But when you ask him, be sure that your faith is in God alone. Do not waver, for a person with divided loyalty is as unsettled as a wave of the sea that is blown and tossed by the wind." This reminds us, we must ask God in faith, without doubting. Ruths know that God is able to do exceedingly abundantly above all they could ask or think, so they trust Him fully to guide and provide.

3. **Confidence:** Ruths believe they can do all things through Christ who strengthens them (Philippians 4:13 "For I can do everything through Christ, who gives me strength."). They know that with God, nothing is

impossible, and they move forward boldly, knowing that He is with them.

4. **Breaking Bondage:** Ruths are committed to breaking the bondage of doubt, insecurity, and the intimidations that society places on women. They do not accept being seen as "less than" but instead embrace their full identity in Christ, knowing they are fearfully and wonderfully made.

Clothing of Confidence

Ruths adorn themselves with confidence, knowing that their worth and strength come from God. When a woman is confident in who she is in Christ, she becomes unstoppable. She does not fear what others say or think because her security is found in the Lord. Like Ruth, she moves forward boldly, breaking barriers and making a significant impact wherever she goes.

Scriptures for Further Study:

1. **Isaiah 43:19**

    "For I am about to do something new. See, I have already begun! Do you not see it? I will make a pathway through the wilderness. I will create rivers in the dry wasteland."

2. **1 Corinthians 16:13**

    "Be on guard. Stand firm in the faith. Be courageous. Be strong."

3. **Romans 8:31**

    "What shall we say about such wonderful things as these? If God is for us, who can ever be against us?"

4. **2 Timothy 1:7**

    "For God has not given us a spirit of fear and timidity, but of power, love, and self-discipline."

5. **Psalm 46:5**

    *"God is within her, she will not fall; God
    will help her at break of day."* (NIV)

6. **Proverbs 31:25**

    *"She is clothed with strength and dignity,
    and she laughs without fear of the future."*

7. **Hebrews 11:1**

    *"Faith shows the reality of what we hope
    for; it is the evidence of things we cannot
    see."*

8. **Joshua 1:9**

    *"This is my command—be strong and
    courageous! Do not be afraid or
    discouraged. For the Lord your God is with
    you wherever you go."*

These scriptures provide further insight into living
as a barrier breaker, embracing a pioneering spirit,
and moving forward confidently in the purposes and
plans that God has for you.

Chapter 7

Virtue

Virtue is defined as "a force to be reckoned with."
It is more than just moral excellence; it includes
qualities like wealth, power, and honor. These
virtues give Ruths the encouragement to push
forward and rebuild broken lives with grace,
strength, and wisdom. Virtue is the foundation upon
which a strong, Godly character is built, allowing us
to stand firm in the face of adversity and shine
brightly in a world that often promotes the opposite.

What Makes Up Virtue?

Virtue is made up of several key qualities:

- **Being Supportive:** Always being there for others, offering help and encouragement.
- **Having Initiative:** Taking the lead in situations where action is needed.
- **Being Enterprising:** Being creative, resourceful, and ready to seize opportunities.
- **Responsibility:** Taking ownership of one's actions and being dependable.
- **Being a Humanitarian:** Caring for others and seeking to improve their lives.
- **Excellent Character:** Striving for honesty, fairness, and moral integrity.
- **Slow to Speak:** Being thoughtful and measured in communication, avoiding rash or harmful words.
- **Strong Nature:** Having resilience and determination, especially in difficult times.
- **Godly Integrity:** Living in alignment with God's principles, maintaining honesty and uprightness in all things.

What Does Gleaning Look Like for You?

In the story of Ruth, gleaning was about working hard in the fields to provide for herself and Naomi. It meant going to the edges of the fields, where the farmers had left grain for the poor to collect. For us today, gleaning might look different but involves the same principles of hard work, humility, and trust in God's provision.

Maybe your gleaning is working for a friend's business or being employed by a family member. Maybe it means stepping out of your comfort zone and trying something new. Just like in Ruth's time, where the poor would gather the leftover grain from the fields to sustain their lives, we must be willing to step out and work hard for what we need. Unlike modern systems that might create dependence without effort, the principle of gleaning is about doing your part and trusting God to provide.

The Key to Success: Faith

The key to being successful is not necessarily how hard you work, but the level of faith you operate in. Do you walk in confidence, believing that God will make a way for you? Do you trust that He will do for you what He has promised? Preparing your heart for success means taking your responsibilities seriously and giving your best in every situation. Let God stretch you, grow your capacity, and lead you from where you are to where He wants you to go.

God Is Stretching You!

Growth involves change, and God often stretches us out of our comfort zones to lead us into a life of significance. This growth can be uncomfortable, but it is necessary for building the kind of character and virtue that God desires in us. Don't be afraid of being stretched — embrace it! God uses these seasons to prepare us for something greater.

Resist the Familiar

Comfort can be an open door for the enemy. When we are too comfortable, we may let our guard down, allowing negative thoughts, habits, or even spiritual attacks to enter our lives. Instead, we must learn to be comfortable with being uncomfortable. Embrace new challenges, trust God to guide you, and remain vigilant in your spiritual journey.

Scriptures for Further Study:

1. **Proverbs 31:10**
    "Who can find a virtuous and capable wife? She is more precious than rubies."

2. **1 Peter 3:4**
    "You should clothe yourselves instead with the beauty that comes from within, the unfading beauty of a gentle and quiet spirit, which is so precious to God."

3. **Philippians 2:3-4**
    "Don't be selfish; don't try to impress others. Be humble, thinking of others as better than yourselves. Don't look out only for your own interests, but take an interest in others, too."

4. **Galatians 6:9**

   "So let's not get tired of doing what is good. At just the right time we will reap a harvest of blessing if we don't give up."

5. **James 1:2-4**

   "Dear brothers and sisters, when troubles of any kind come your way, consider it an opportunity for great joy. For you know that when your faith is tested, your endurance has a chance to grow. So let it grow, for when your endurance is fully developed, you will be perfect and complete, needing nothing."

6. **Romans 5:3-4**

   "We can rejoice, too, when we run into problems and trials, for we know that they help us develop endurance. And endurance develops strength of character, and character strengthens our confident hope of salvation."

7. **Proverbs 12:4**

   "A worthy wife is a crown for her husband, but a disgraceful woman is like cancer in his bones."

8. **Ephesians 6:10-11**

   "A final word: Be strong in the Lord and in his mighty power. Put on all of God's armor so that you will be able to stand firm against all strategies of the devil."

9. **Colossians 3:23-24**

   "Work willingly at whatever you do, as though you were working for the Lord rather than for people. Remember that the Lord will give you an inheritance as your reward, and that the Master you are serving is Christ."

10. **Isaiah 40:31**

    "But those who trust in the Lord will find new strength. They will soar high on wings like eagles. They will run and not grow weary. They will walk and not faint."

These scriptures help us understand how virtue builds a strong character that glorifies God and inspires others. They encourage us to press on in faith, resist the comfort of familiarity, and embrace the challenges that come our way as opportunities to grow and glorify God.

Chapter 8

Vindication and Re-established

Ruths Are Different:

Ruths are set apart and distinct in many ways. They come from diverse backgrounds and are not of the same household — they are Gentiles, adopted by grace into God's family. They come from different paths in life, but they look at affluence as a tool, not a goal. They are morally stable, possess excellent character, and demonstrate uncompromising honor in everything they do. They reflect the grace of God in their lives, showing that it is not where you come from, but who you choose to follow that truly matters.

The Threshing Floor

The **threshing floor** is a powerful symbol in Ruth's story. It represents a place of separation and decision, where childless widows could have their deceased husbands' estates redeemed by a close relative, as described in **Deuteronomy 25:5-10** "If two brothers are living together on the same property, and one of them dies without a son, his widow may not be married to anyone from outside the family. Instead, her husband's brother should marry her and have intercourse with her to fulfill the duties of a brother-in-law. The first son she bears to him will be considered the son of the dead brother, so that his name will not be forgotten in Israel. But if the man refuses to marry his brother's widow, she must go to the town gate and say to the elders assembled there, 'My husband's brother refuses to preserve his brother's name in Israel—he refuses to fulfill the duties of a brother-in-law by marrying me.' The elders of the town will then summon him and talk with him. If he still refuses and says, 'I don't want to marry her,' the widow must walk over to him in the presence of the elders, pull his sandal from his foot, and spit in his face. Then she must declare, 'This is what happens to a man who refuses to provide his brother with children.'"

For Ruth, the threshing floor was where she approached Boaz, seeking redemption and a new beginning. It is a place where we are called to separate from the past and prepare ourselves for what God has in store.

Preparation Needed:

1. **Wash Yourself:**

   o **Physically and Spiritually:** Physical washing was necessary for Ruth to be found clean and appealing to her redeemer, Boaz. Spiritually, this represents washing away the death of the past and renewing ourselves in a fresh relationship with God. This is a process of sanctification, setting ourselves apart for God's use.

2. **Anoint Yourself:**

   o **Set Apart for Holy Use:** Anointing is a symbol of being set apart for God's purposes. It breaks the power of the flesh, aligning our thoughts and hearts with God's will.

3. **Wear Your Best:**

   o **Deliberately Letting Go of the Past:** Ruth dressed in her best clothes as a sign of moving forward, leaving the past behind, and preparing herself for a new season.

4. **At the Threshing Floor:**

   o **A Place of Separation:** The threshing floor is where we must let go of the past and remove any hindrance that keeps us separated from God. Only then can we enter a new level with Him.

○ **Putting Down the Old to Take Up the New:** At this place, we lay down old relationships, past anointings, and outdated mindsets to embrace new relationships, a fresh anointing, a renewed mind, a new heart, and new assignments from God.

Restoring Ancient Pathways

Restoring ancient pathways involves seeking a godly covering — a protector, provider, spouse, and husband. Ruth followed the instructions given to her, adhering to Jewish culture and tradition. She submitted to the process and trusted God with the outcome.

What Does the Threshing Floor Represent?

1. **Shedding the Old, Keeping the New:** The threshing floor is where the grain is

separated from the chaff. It symbolizes letting go of what is no longer needed and holding onto what is valuable.

2. **Irritation to Healing:** It is a place where the friction and pressure of the past are transformed into a new beginning and healing.

3. **Covenant Commitment:** In Ruth 3:9, when Ruth says, "Spread the hem of your garment over me," she is asking Boaz for protection and a covenant commitment of marriage.

4. **Security:** The threshing floor is a place where God provides security and stability for those who trust in Him.

5. **Trust in the Redeemer:** It is where we learn to trust fully in God, our Redeemer, who watches over us and provides for all our needs.

Restoring Ancient Pathways

Restoring ancient pathways also means accessing the provision of God, our Provider. It is tapping into the treasury of heaven, not according to our desires, but as the Lord sees fit to provide for the needs of His children. God is faithful to His Word, and He will always fulfill His promises. Proverbs 6:31 tells us, *"But if he is caught, he must pay back seven times what he stole, even if he has to sell everything in his house."* This speaks of God's justice and restoration, where the enemy who steals must repay sevenfold — a symbol of God's perfect restoration.

This book of Ruth is not a love story in the way we might read in a romantic novel. It is a story of God's unwavering love for all humanity, His sons, and daughters. Israel was the beginning of God's plan, and He will not stop until the whole world understands and has the chance to accept His great love of redemption.

What Is Your Threshing Floor Experience?

Your threshing floor experience is your personal journey of letting go of the old to embrace the new. It is where God completes your recovery, restoration, and resurrection in Him so that you can receive your inheritance in the Lord. Ultimately, this inheritance is eternity in heaven. Allow God to unlock His greatness, tenacity, and destiny within you. Trust Him to guide you through the process, knowing that He is faithful to finish the work He has started in you.

Scriptures for Further Study:

1. **Deuteronomy 25:5-10**
   "If two brothers are living together on the same property, and one of them dies without a son, his widow may not be married to anyone from outside the family. Instead, her husband's brother should marry her and have intercourse with her to fulfill the duties of a brother-in-law. The first son she bears to him will be considered the son of the dead brother, so that his name will not be forgotten in Israel. But if the man refuses to marry his brother's widow, she must go to the town gate and say to the elders assembled there, 'My husband's brother refuses to preserve his brother's name in Israel—he refuses to fulfill the duties of a

brother-in-law by marrying me.' The elders of the town will then summon him and talk with him. If he still refuses and says, 'I don't want to marry her,' the widow must walk over to him in the presence of the elders, pull his sandal from his foot, and spit in his face. Then she must declare, 'This is what happens to a man who refuses to provide his brother with children.'"

2.   **Ruth 3:9**
     "'Who are you?' he asked. 'I am your servant Ruth,' she replied. 'Spread the corner of your covering over me, for you are my family redeemer.'"

3.   **Proverbs 6:31**
     "But if he is caught, he must pay back seven times what he stole, even if he has to sell everything in his house."

4.   **Isaiah 61:7**
     "Instead of shame and dishonor, you will enjoy a double share of honor. You will possess a double portion of prosperity in your land, and everlasting joy will be yours."

5. **Psalm 37:4**

    "Take delight in the Lord, and he will give you your heart's desires."

6. **Joel 2:25**

    "The Lord says, 'I will give you back what you lost to the swarming locusts, the hopping locusts, the stripping locusts, and the cutting locusts. It was I who sent this great destroying army against you.'"

7. **Psalm 51:10**

    "Create in me a clean heart, O God. Renew a loyal spirit within me."

8. **Romans 8:28**

    "And we know that God causes everything to work together for the good of those who love God and are called according to his purpose for them."

9. **2 Corinthians 5:17**

    "This means that anyone who belongs to Christ has become a new person. The old life is gone; a new life has begun!"

10. **Isaiah 43:18-19**

    "But forget all that — it is nothing

compared to what I am going to do. For I
am about to do something new. See, I have
already begun! Do you not see it? I will
make a pathway through the wilderness. I
will create rivers in the dry wasteland."

These scriptures provide deeper insights into God's redemptive power, His ability to restore what was lost, and His promise of new beginnings for those who trust in Him. They emphasize the themes of sanctification, renewal, divine provision, and God's unfailing love and justice.

These scriptures provide a deeper understanding of redemption, restoration, and trusting in God's plan for our lives, as well as the importance of preparation and sanctification in our journey of faith.

Conclusion: Embracing the Ruth Anointing

The journey of Ruth is one of transformation, from a place of brokenness to a position of honor and restoration. Her story begins with loss and grief, but it evolves into one of redemption, love, and divine purpose. Ruth exemplifies dedication, faithfulness, and an unyielding trust in God's plan. Her journey from Moab to Bethlehem mirrors our own spiritual journeys — moving from places of comfort, or even desolation, into a land of promise and purpose.

Ruth's loyalty to God, demonstrated through her unwavering commitment to Naomi, shows us the power of covenant relationships. She leaves behind her homeland and her former gods, fully embracing the God of Israel. This kind of loyalty, devotion, and submission to the Holy Spirit is what God seeks from each of us. It requires us to let go of the past, trust in His plan, and move forward with courage and determination, no matter the cost.

As we've explored in these chapters, the "Ruth Anointing" is not merely about following a set of rules or performing good deeds; it is about embracing a lifestyle of integrity, humility, and courage. Ruth's example teaches us to break the barriers that society places on us, to step boldly into new territory, and to trust in God's provision and timing. It calls us to walk in our divine purpose with the same pioneering spirit that Ruth exhibited — one that opens new ground and never shrinks back in fear.

Ruth shows us that true strength lies not in our ability to control our circumstances but in our willingness to surrender to God's greater plan. She was a barrier breaker — breaking the back of poverty, gender bias, and societal limitations. Her faith and determination were evident in her actions;

she wasn't content to remain idle or fearful. Instead, she trusted that God would make a way and was prepared to do her part in His unfolding plan.

Throughout this journey, we've seen the importance of virtue in the life of a Ruth. Virtue is more than just moral excellence; it is a force that propels us forward and empowers us to rebuild broken lives. A virtuous person is supportive, responsible, and strong in character, embodying godly integrity. Ruth's virtue made her a woman of strength and purpose, someone who was both humble and courageous, always ready to step out in faith.

Ruth's story is also a powerful reminder of God's vindication and re-establishment. Even though she came from a different background, as a Moabite, she was adopted by grace into the family of God. At the threshing floor, Ruth demonstrated humility and boldness, seeking redemption and restoration for herself and Naomi. God honored her faith and commitment, restoring not only her personal life but also the ancient pathways of His people, leading directly to the lineage of King David and ultimately to Jesus Christ.

The experiences at the threshing floor are symbolic of the spiritual process we must all undergo. It is a place where we let go of the old, where what is unnecessary is separated from what is vital. It is where we are washed, anointed, and prepared for the new things God has for us. Like Ruth, we must go through the process of sanctification, shedding our old selves, and putting on the new identities God has given us in Christ.

The life of Ruth challenges us to ask, "What is our threshing floor experience?" Are we willing to be cleansed, sanctified, and prepared for a greater purpose? Are we ready to trust God fully, even when the path is unclear? Ruth's example shows us that if we endure the process, God will bring about our recovery, restoration, and resurrection in Him. He will unlock His greatness and destiny within us, leading us toward our ultimate inheritance — eternal life with Him.

Ultimately, the story of Ruth is a reflection of God's unwavering love and commitment to redeem and restore all of humanity. It reminds us that no matter our background, past mistakes, or present challenges, God's grace is sufficient. He sees us, knows us, and has a plan to bring us into His purpose. He is our Redeemer, and in Him, we find true security, provision, and peace.

May we all embrace the Ruth anointing in our lives. May we be women and men of courage, faith, and integrity, committed to God's call and willing to break every barrier that stands in the way of His divine purposes. Let us step boldly into the new things God has for us, trusting that His plans are always for our good and His glory. As Ruth's life shows, when we commit ourselves fully to God, He will use us in ways that exceed our greatest expectations, fulfilling His perfect will in and through us.

Bibliography

Primary Sources:

1. **The Holy Bible, New Living Translation (NLT).**
   Used for all scripture references and interpretations,
   providing the biblical foundation for the themes and
   lessons in chapters 1-8. Key passages include:
   - Ruth 1-4 (The story of Ruth and Naomi)
   - John 14:16-17 (The Holy Spirit as a Helper)
   - Proverbs 3:5-6 (Trust in the Lord)
   - Isaiah 50:7 (Strength and determination in
     the Lord)
   - 1 John 4:18 (Perfect love casting out fear)
   - Deuteronomy 25:5-10 (Laws regarding
     redemption and levirate marriage)
   - Philippians 4:13 (Strength through Christ)
   - Proverbs 31:10 (Virtue and value of a
     woman)

Additional Scriptures Referenced:

2. **Book of Proverbs:**

   - Proverbs 6:31, Proverbs 11:14, Proverbs
     17:17, Proverbs 22:11 (Wisdom, guidance,
     and covenant relationships)

3. **Book of Isaiah:**

- o   Isaiah 43:18-19, Isaiah 46:10, Isaiah 61:7 (God's promises, restoration, and new beginnings)

4. **Book of Psalms:**

- o   Psalm 37:4, Psalm 37:23-24, Psalm 46:5, Psalm 51:10, Psalm 133:1 (God's guidance, virtue, strength, and unity)

5. **New Testament Letters:**

- o   James 1:5-6 (Wisdom and faith), Romans 8:28 (God's purpose for good), 1 Corinthians 1:10 (Unity in the body of Christ), Galatians 6:9 (Perseverance in doing good), Colossians 3:14 (Love and harmony)

6. **Other Biblical Texts:**

- o   Deuteronomy 32:30 (God's power in unity), Ecclesiastes 4:9-10 (Value of partnership), Joshua 1:9 (Courage in God's presence), Hebrews 10:24-25 (Encouragement and community)

Secondary Sources:

7. **Commentaries and Theological Texts:**

- o   **"Matthew Henry's Commentary on the Whole Bible."** Matthew Henry. (Classic commentary providing historical and theological insights into the Book of Ruth and related scriptures)

- o **"The New Bible Commentary."** Edited by G.J. Wenham, J.A. Motyer, D.A. Carson, and R.T. France. (Provides academic insights and context for understanding the story of Ruth and its application to contemporary life)

8. **Books on Christian Living and Spiritual Growth:**

- o **"The Ruth Anointing: Becoming a Woman of Faith, Virtue, and Destiny."** Michelle McClain-Walters. (Explores the life of Ruth as a model for women today, encouraging them to embrace a calling of faith, virtue, and purpose)
- o **"Women of the Bible: A One-Year Devotional Study of Women in Scripture."** Ann Spangler and Jean E. Syswerda. (Provides daily devotionals and studies on the lives of biblical women, including Ruth)

Articles and Online Resources:

9. **"Character Studies: Ruth."** Bible Study Tools. Accessed online for historical and cultural context surrounding Ruth's life and the Book of Ruth.

10. **"Understanding Biblical Covenants."** Christianity.com. Accessed for detailed explanations

of covenant relationships in the Bible and their applications in the modern Christian life.

Author's Note:

These resources were consulted to provide a deeper understanding of the themes, cultural context, and theological insights presented in chapters 1-8 of this book. The primary reliance has been on the biblical text itself, with secondary sources serving to enhance and clarify the interpretation and application of Scripture.

Our Contact Information, Channels, and Booklist

CONTACT US AT: SHREADAMBASSADORS@GMAIL.COM

CHANNELS BY PASTOR BETH KELLEY:
PASTOR CHANNEL: http://
www.youtube.com@JIGSAWPastorBeth
Jesus Is Gathering Saints Around the World
CRAFTING CHANNEL: http://www.youtube.com/
@pearltreasuredesigns.
OUR LIFE CHANNEL: http://www.youtube.com/
@kellsshenanigans

CONTACT US AT: SHREADAMBASSADORS@GMAIL.COM

BOOK TITLES BY DOROFIA ISLOVE:
Coloring Book: Whispers of Faith in Natures Paradise, A
Journey of Relaxation and Reflection.
Coloring Book: Animals Around the World & Nature Scenes

Recipe Book: Deliciously Inspired: Home Cooking

Timing Is Everything, *A Journey of Patience, Growth and Resilience*

BOOK TITLES BY PASTOR BETH KELLEY:
Sarah: A Woman of Faith
Sarah: A Woman of Faith Study Guide
Sarah: A Woman of Faith Teachers Guide
Sarah: A Woman of Faith 365 Day Devotional
From Barrenness to Breakthrough, "Trusting God's Plan For
Your Life"
Faith & Courage, *Emma and Max's Journey Through Life's Toughest Challenges*

BOOK TITLES BY PASTOR CHARLENE TUCKER:
God Wants You!
God Wants You! Study Guide
God Wants You! Teacher Edition Study Guide

Arise: Embracing Your Divine Destiny! "Stories of Faith, Strength, and Unity for Young Women"
Arise: Young Hearts Embracing God's Plan. "Stories of Faith, Strength, and Unity for Young Girls"

Mindful coloring book for Adults
God's Precious Princesses: A Coloring Book of Love and Affirmations
God's Big Adventures: A Coloring Book with Trucks, Trains, and Planes
Whimsical Wings: A Crazy Bird Coloring Adventure
"Coloring God's Truth: Affirmations for Brave and Blessed Kids"

MINI BRAIN CHALLENGES PUZZLE BOOKS

Unfolding Truth Empowering Men
Unfolding Truth Journals

Find Us On Amazon by typing the Author's Name in the search bar.

Made in the USA
Columbia, SC
23 June 2025

59660257R00052